A Renaissance Woman's Musings on Black Excellence

Anne Desrosiers

BookLeaf
Publishing

India | USA | UK

Presentation by *BookLeaf Publishing*

Web: www.bookleafpub.com

E-mail: info@bookleafpub.com

ISBN: 9789360940713

First edition 2024

To my boys, Lucas & Marceau, thank you for giving me continued motivation to hope for a better world, excuses to continue on adventures of a lifetime in the small wonders of every day and the ball outs around the world.

Always remember the sky is the limit and your joy needs to be fiercely protected and defended.

ACKNOWLEDGEMENT

Committing to the creative process consistently is one of the hardest things to do. Especially when trying to adult, parent, partner, and friend.

However, if we release the pressure we put on ourselves to meet arbitrary deadlines, we'll realize that most of us have committed. We just didn't consistently zoom out and reflect enough to realize that the evidence is scattered in all the facets of our lives.

I was able to unearth thanks to the inspiration of some of the most creative and talented people I have the pleasure of knowing and seeing them commit to create. So to my Chicago girls: Cassie, Lenora, and Stephanie thanks and keep going :-)
And special mention to my (Birthday) Twin Lori who shares each iteration in waays that continue to inspire me.

Lastly, to Papa Bean, for always making sure you're Dadding 10,000 so I have the space to honor the commitment to keep creating. Love you all.

Thank you for taking the time to read my poetry.
I hope it gives me the honor of being your fave
Dr.

Dr. Anne

PREFACE

Living through so much, how do we internalize and process the hopes we have for life? As a Xennial and 80s Baby it feels like we can't catch a break!

Some of these writings reflect that hopeless feeling that the sky IS falling, and so these feelings need to get OUT.

While others were written when I first put pen to paper trying to make sense of the meanings of life, and how ordinary experiences transcend as great metaphors for where we are now.

For me, these are musings in the truest sense. An inside look at the artistic rationalization of life: back then, and now in its myriad of latitudes and longitudes.

Back, to the Present

From my public school days it was mostly
straight As...
The teachers always looked out, "inquisitive,
talkative, sociable"
THIS immigrant's child shouldn't go astray

Now, in the DEI sessions I lead, there's this
power & privilege wheel
All the karens & kens riled the fuck up: at the
truth that they are at the center
While our ENTIRE struggles, our entire lives,
OUR FEELS, is not even a (small) deal

From my Ivy League, undergrad days it was out
of body, TV show, spectated
Blanquitos partaking in snow, hanging upside
down in alcohol in vats
Somehow though, the merits of our admission,
what silver spoon feeds denigrated

Now, I hold a PhD yes! THE highest degree!
Still remember one of my fave English
professor's chat
When she opined in a British accent "You're
bright but you can't write" told to MEE

From my first foray at adulting: job-hunting—a
small typo in my email
And a basic, pasty, clear dude went CLEAR off
about my Ivy degree & said typo
Saddest part is his soapbox was a pedestal from
a temp agency, so I ain't fail

Now, the excuses for not proofreading: "excuse
any typos sent from mobile"
Busting my ass HARD to pay on time, to BE
ON TIME, and get some credit —
The mediocre, made up, imaginary, system
BEAST so DAMN formidable

From my grad school group project where I
played to my strengths
Held it down, did key work: only for a
"teammate" to "word-vomit' to prof.
SNAP: no more trust for me office, hours so
what? Ain't no coming off THAT fence

Now, I make sure to watch like a hawk the
places my sons play
They're cute now, but that time is upon us &
everything is dialing back
Everything they ever think about US makes their
SHIT okay

From elementary school when they would call
my Peyisans Haitian Bootyscratchr
To when the Asian lady tried to play my Home
Health Aide Mom
Her daughter denied admission from the same
Ivy, my essay was THE factor

Now, I take stock of how random and yet
specific people try to play in my face
Black on black robbery cuz I'm just a
multi-talented mom, trying to make a $1
When the women highest up in Ed, cant utter
pronoun DR. I give them grace

From when I realized my God-given calling, in
the pursuit of passion
Traveling & teaching: life BEEN lifin' guess
energy runs off more than sweat
God said that light is darkness' main attraction

Now I stay prayed up, looking around at the
fallacies of the empire
Making sure I don't let the beast fuck with me,
not no more
They not quick enough for that championship
hold-time SWAGGER

From Flatbush, the hydrant on hot summer days

Manmi's doing what they need to to pave aa way
for without partners, spouses
4th of July illegal FIRECRACKERS, New
Year's Day gun play

Now I count countries, read affirmations, clean
& consult my altar
The prodigal daughter stayed close, despite
constant snares of the SSSNAKE
My legacy is praying me and mines, though we
waiver don't falter

Captain America

"ANGRY!!" A threat to the Efficient,
Ever-so-benevolent Government!

"Pull yourselves UP! By your bootstraps!!" Just
NOT with your fellow man,
ESPECIALLY if relying on the Efficient,
Ever-so-benevolent Government!!

You don't deserve! Not that promotion,
DEFINITELY NOT, Not that pay raise AND:
By the way: train your manager-supervisor while
keeping company boast adrift.

You don't deserve! To be Yourself, because WE.
. . don't. . . get it? "That's so ghetto, NO
CLASS!" "What's with the HAIR? What's with
the lingo. . .it's so LIT?
Is that how you use it? Let me steal it, it's so
fetch. . .in (only) THESE ways!!
Come braid my kids' hair just like that, Ghetto,
when we get those temp melanin tags annd
VROOOM-VROOM like vultures while on
vacation, or in foreign.

"ANGRY!!" A threat to our mediocrity& how
DARE YOU speak up?
Speak back to a public macro (but we like
"micro") aggression. Appalling: that's not the
culture here, we are like FAMILY (except you're
not *really* one of us)!

Save us!! Vote like your lives depended on it.
And vote like THIS so we can pass...
Mmmm actually play ping-pong or rather
pickle-ball!! It's all the rage, much slower and
our pace of change ya know!

You don't deserve! Oh and DON'T BY ANY
MEANS NECESSARY support your own.
We don't REALLY mean PULL YOURSELVES
UP! That's discrimination against US!

Save us!! What's new in the culture? What's the
latest dance that is BEGGING for mayonnaise
takes & plagiarism swipes that are the
descendants of "Discovery"
And WE built THIS right here, yall were just
extras? Props? Production assistants? One of
these WILL work!

"ANGRY!!" It's not MY FAULT I have
privilege! You don't work HARD enough-BUT

Wipe my baby's, my mom's, my dad's, and MY
ass on demand. Cuz this hard-EARNED six
figures for this too-big house was rightly
acquired and MUST be maintained

You don't deserve! Justice when your kids,
brothers, mothers, sisters, cousins get lynched on
handheld screens. Respect for life is for those
who OBEY THE LAW! Blue Lives Matter!
Comply—we just don't know all the facts.

"ANGRY!!" Don't emote, don't feel, despite
being 10x as good since you had to be
Better for about 5 more years to be seen. You
should be grateful for this nomination! Be
grateful when you lose, put on a happy face!
Because The Academy is your pinnacle! Was
she a slave, a bed wench, a stereotype we LOVE
to see though?

Save us!! Do OUR dirty work and accept it.
Always be the one
Who talks us out of our demons on scree or in
real time:
Reflect Satan as policy as our beards

You don't deserve! The shield, the cape, the
tights.

Captain America was (without you of course)
always gonna be ALRIGHT

The Impressions of Motherhood

Wake up and on this, like most AMs
if it's quiet, there's respite
A few moments for self—gathered
like the brush strokes attempting to create the
'perfect' shade?

What is time? Her portrait once a vision of one,
somewhat?
Monochromatic texture. . .Routine, the repetitive
cadence does that. . .
makes time feel hum-drum, yet vibrant at times
with ripples of newness,
uncertainty, change. . .

Her craft of self & personhood once well
defined, sharp, poignant—
now an Impressionist piece—seemingly
unfinished
parts unblended, the essence still there but a
constant mirroring of former
and discovering

How does the new and constant light in her life
change & ebb over the course

of the day(s)? In this moment—it's the silent
reading of a scripture
"Eh-eh; ehh-ehh... Waaaaahhhhhh!"
The moment ends & the artwork of motherhood
continues. . .

Fall (And I)

The autumn foilage harkens me to get the boots.
The leaves orange hues coax out the trench.
Like a cornucopia colorful centerpiece,
I layer the scarves, the sweaters, the mauve lip

Although death is a never-ending invisible
cloak—
the harvest proves, somehow, someway there's
still growth to be found
The trunks sprout branches,
buds begin to form or shed their roasted edges

It's a good season mixed like epis:
with some bright notes and zesty peaks
But mellow enough to be simple when it needs
to be

A shift in two worlds, the joy of the season
flashes like a peacock's tail
But definitely one of celebration,
of all the good and wealth it beholds

I Am

I am a visionary and a changemaker
I wonder when my dreams will take flight
I hear wings clapping in the wind
I see my dreams flying high
I want to make a difference

I am a leader and a general
I pretend to order the troops
I feel like a commander in chief
I touch my badge of courage
I worry that my dreams may not soar
I cry when I think about not sharing the results
of my dreams with my mother

I am a visionary and a changemaker
I understand it starts with me
I say an army of one is powerful
I dream about life once my dreams take off

I try to fake it until I make it
I hope I make it
I am a visionary and a changemaker

A Treatise to (Black) Kids in Murica, And To My Sons

I love you. And while EVERYONE says yall are
"SO CAYUTE!"
The time is fast approaching when you won't be.
When people will see you, my children, as
adults.
When they'll pretend that you're a menace, a
threat, a danger.
Even as you do things kids should and would do.

All I see are your smiles, your loving eyes.
I feel your innocence, your hugs, your joy.
The way everything is new, the wonder, the
curiosity of a different place.
Fiercely protecting that, I know all too well
what's to come.

How do I prepare you for THAT world?
What can I do to be your cloak of armor?
What happens when I, your fierce defender, can't
avenge the ills of the world?
How can I make sure remnants of your budding
foundation remain firm?
The legacy I am trying to establish takes root for
you, and your children?

I can teach, help you understand the valuable
things
Pray that even with these tools—the world
doesn't swallow you whole,
mistaking you for something you're not.
Beg that injustice doesn't take you too soon,
before God calls you home.

A Treatise to my sons and the (Black) kids in
'Murica:
Because the quiet and loud part is your race.
They can see it on your face, but they'll pretend
they don't
They will give every reason besides THAT for
the multitude of wrongs

Stolen ideas, sabotaged work, harsher
punishments, false accusations.
Tread every so lightly with the company you
keep.
You can be damaged, discarded collateral for
any stupid reason—
Your life snuffed out because of white tears,
white-washed machinations

Their system and their people operate together
loudly.

Showing you how they see you, keep watch!
Eyes—OPEN, opinions: MUTE
Keep vigilant like a lighthouse observatory
ALWAYS ON SWIVEL
They quietly avoid any accountability,
knowledge, or recognizance
Learn the professional language to play on the
board, vocabulary is your friend

A Treatise to my sons and the (Black) kids in
'Murica:
Because even if we raised you privileged, you're
already behind.
They don't want you to win, and place traps
along the way
Take heed, press on

A dollar towards debts paid, is a dollar towards
freedom
Ownership is key, don't fall prey to the floss!
Credit is a mirage, knowing you paid the bills is
worth its weight in (white) gold

Always know where your dollar is going and
who your spending supports
It don't never NEED to be designer, esp. when
you research what they stand on
If it is designer, always on discount and only if
you paid in full

A Treatise to my sons and the (Black) kids in
'Murica:
Because the things we knew made a life for you.
Our only vision was for you to stand on what we
did
Be better, go higher and know that

Self-sufficiency=TRUE independence
Both me + Daddy can cook, more than just on
the stove
Have skills and knowledge; study yourself and
your interests
That always PAYS

Most can't do what you KNOW—but
will use your Time, Talent & Energy (TTE) for
self
Because they don't appreciate the real VALUE
of you
Know yourself, know your worth, and become
an expert before you add tax

Everything in its place, and a place for
everything
Adulting is an exercise in organization,
Success is an exercise of freedom, and your
OWN belief of "making it'

Real gangstas move in silence,
But there's always a time to mobilize for causes
greater than yourself
Build your army over the years, note the solid
ones who stay the course
Conflict arises, criticism is normal—be above
conflict and within criticism
Constantly developing, master your mind—mind
your manners

Be strong in faith, find it, feel it, live it
We built a life source of joy for you because we
are believers
The highest powers are not of this world and the
ancestors keep us
Honor your culture and that of your parents for
the lessons & protections

Tune out the noise, tune into self, never follow
the crowd
It's okay to say "I don't know" just be sure to
figure it out, if its important enough
Ikigai: Love your life even in the valleys
Happiness is created, seek it out and always
explore
New places, new things, eyes open = MIND
OPEN

A Treatise to my sons and the (Black) kids in
'Murica:
Because I won't always be here, and my love can
only go so far.
You're not mine, you're your own person I'm just
the guardian of your journey
I was not always sage, but I do my best

Life is never without its roadblocks, hardships,
and hard truths
I will always be rooting for you my children
Despite what the world sees, I will always see
your ascent as rising, shining stars
God made you in His image and I am always in
dedication to your fulfillment
The world be damned

Social Media

Tap, tap, scroll...
Like reality TV, the senselessness of the scroll is
an addiction
I know there is plenty on my to do list, and yet. .
.
I just want to do this. . .

Tap, tap, scroll...
The news of the day, ever since Shaun King's
been banned
There's some semblance of less knowing
The genocide was live, for us Blacks (and
browns) it's always been televised
Is it escapism? Am I really out?
This version of the Matrix may be the central
plot

Tap, tap, scroll...
Do you want to make six figures?
You NEED to make six figures!
Nah, matter of fact you need a MILLION PLUS
Having an event that isn't grandiose you might
just go nuts!

Tap, tap, scroll...

Culture wars, internally between us the beef is
biggest
Loudest voices are ignorance, Black
Twitter—now X
Couldn't make $500 out of fifteen hundred
cents...:steups: talking about edges
Black women need to be more SUBMISSIVE,
Black men are the most attacked!
Girls gone wild, ape-shit, crazy on another
bullshit podcast

Tap, Tap, Scroll...
Wake up! First things, first, make sure to see
what's happenin'
Not talking to the Lord, not to say grace, but the
app is uploading me
Downloading the latest messaging, the modus
operandi of the day
How much time has gone by?
Head buried, in this virtual insanity

Tap, Tap, Scroll...
If they haven't seen it, its not real
If it's not a link in bio, do you actually do it?
30 second stories, 90 second reels, average
watch time 60 seconds
The degrees splayed on walls, real life, work
done

Is it on your page? What's your handle?
Highlights, to which we've all succumb

Tap, tap, scroll...
I need to get out, this can't be life
But this food looks so beautiful!
I need others to see it! Experiencing with
screens, and semblances of community
A few people reached out, they haven't noticed
me on Facebook
Damn, at least I'm remembered random thoughts
taking space in a digital nook

Tap, tap, scroll...
Despite the censorship, and the call for our own
platform
It already exists, but THAT news didn't spread?
Another uphill battle...
For us, by us, drowned out in the wave
Launching a new business and have to create
another page
Social media lives to see another indoctrinated
day

Dystopia's Utopia

After NY's Blizzard of '96 it was a good run!
Most of my youth unscathed by the promises of
"The American Dream," going to school, getting
good grades
allllll that model immigrant behavior.

Graduated 2007, headed to my top choice.
Made it from public school to the Ivy League!
Truth be told I didn't see myself as a unicorn
then
I was just a smart (and poor—hey scholarship!)
Black girl,
who had sound college counseling, a mean work
ethic, and a desire to be there

On campus, affirmative action on the chopping
block
The silver spoon conglomerate the antithesis of
all that I had done,
questioning mine, (and other very intelligent
Black people's) merits
Fellow classmates descending upon the halls of
Ben Franklin's institution
with leg ups taller than giraffes it seemed.

Their programs preparing them for moneyed
scenes...
of alcoholism, coke-dealing, and
still—questioning merits.
Questioning myself, my class and my
worth—albeit briefly.

The stares, the comments in class. "I don't speak
for all Black people"
Making sure to handle MY business and worry
about surviving those first semesters as a
freshman with some mirage of achievement
looming .
Despite the numerical—is this accurate (maybe
it's false?) equivalent.
I've never been here before—But I am here!
Making it, more than some my of other
classmates who transferred,
went crazy, left under the stressors and duress of
other people's utopia.

The academic utopia wealthy and elite are
DYING for their kids to be at.
C-list celebrities pay and scam for less than MY,
very own, minted
Baccalaureus Artium. I made it! I survived and
even thrived at the end of 4 years.

Feeling good, looking for work. Temp tp perm,
the way to get IN BABY!
SCCRREEEECCCCCHHHHHHHHHHHHHHH!
The grinding halt of the Great Recession of '08
stops any semblance of a salary
First on the chopping block, I was laid off when
automation took my job revising real estate ads
for newspapers. Sounds kinda like Mad Men
anyway.
Good thing I was going to grad school to make a
difference...
shielded for some time while the dystopia of no
money, no work, no prospects
loomed even longer than the initial stand-still.

One cross-country move, no full-time teaching
gig later, driving back
Minimum wage the lifeline—as a Volunteer In
Service to America dystopia.
Captain Planet would be proud! My mom,
well—these things take time...
Not a "good job," but a path forward, in a sector.
"Step-by-step // Day-by-day // A fresh start over
// A different hand to play //
The deeper we fall // The stronger we stay"
That was my show coming up! If only I had
come from a Full House
I wouldn't be renting a room before my mom
coerced me to "Vin dormi deye do'm" "Come

sleep behind my back" Save money, moved back
home

Felt like losing my privacy was the worst of the
dystopia—
But have you ever lived with a Haitian mommy
or better yet an auntie?
They say adults shouldn't live together...and
well...that's probably true
Found my stride after asserting myself as an
adult who just couldn't catch a break
Also giving grace for my role as their dream
deferred, there to assist—
instead of drying up like a raisin in the sun.

Homeownership, 5 years after moving back
home. Utopia.
This mine! The peace, the quiet. "Said we're
movin on up! Movin on up!"
Those years were great. Except changing
schools to make more money, only to...
be on the verge of depression, exhausted, under
appreciated, attacked.
All for teaching, with conviction, but the hood
just didn't deserve me no more.
The segregated, educational & systemic
dystopia.
Performance improvement plan—"you're tone is
problematic."

I ain't going out like this.

Broke free, earned my PhD. Paid up that
mortgage for a few before shit got real.
Freedom's utopia. Crazy that it took my whole
life to be "middle class."
Only for "middle class" to be the Sisyphian rock.
Clawed my way to maintaining freedom,
pushing the rock.
SCCRREEEECCCCCHHHHHHHHHHHHHH!
The grinding halt of a global pandemic, another
layoff for me.

Utopia. Everything closed, no baby shower—but
love still.
Sent in the form of boxes, gifts on the porch.
The pod my mom's in Brooklyn, growing life,
taking it all in.
Outside walks: me, my man, and our baby.
Perspective utopia. THIS is what matters.
Dystopia, no hospital visits (they think Long
Island is Afghanistan anyway).
Utopia, the post-op DJ battle we had, while
waiting
to get sensation back in my feet
Dystopia, our NICU baby—one visitor at a time,
no cuddles
Going home without him, same schedule—apart
not together

Utopia: tiny feet, tiny hands, milestones even
more pronounced.
People actually wanted pictures and looked at
our baby bean! AWWWWWW.
The Quiet Time outside, a reminder that:
"It could all be so simple, plain, plain, plain; But
you'd rather make it hard"
Capitalism dead ass cap

Utopia: my 3rd born rainbow baby, all the
celebration—privately though
Baby moon, entrepreneurship, in bloom...then
BOOOOOOOOOM!!!!
Bombs over Gaza. In real time the Holocaust.
2.0 right in our faces
Killing babies and children for oil, land, and the
war machine stocks
The same resources they've been controlling
Dystopia: crying for children I don't know,
mothers I've never met

Dystopia: The Congo & Sudan— the continent
never been free
Slavery rages on: the women, the children still
being raped
For the sake of our lecherous relations with the
latest and greatest tech
I thought climate change was a "priority"...

Weren't they supposed to be moving away from
fossil fuels?
Capitalism kills and it takes presidents aways
too #FreeHaiti

Dystopia, just another notch in the days that feel
like the end of days
They don't want us to say "Free Palestine"
215 bodies in a mass grave down south in
Mississippi
What future will there be for my sons?

Utopia: protecting Black Boy Joy.
Their smiles; having dance parties; making
memories.
Loving up on my Chocolate Drop: Black Love is
Revolutionary
Making strides to be better than we were.
Seeing the world with my boys.

Dystopia's Utopia: life in a self-curated bubble;
freedom from the noise

The Window

Dreams are a window to our desires
It's like we get what we really want and get to
really explore our fire
When we zone out and go into that other world
Sometimes it can't be explained—which is how
our destiny unfurls

Dreams are the key to the real reality, away from
lived reality
Destiny is what we're meant to become and what
is meant to be
Dreams and destiny are one in the same
symbolically
For we can equally control the outcome of both
if we wish to be free

The outlets of our wants, the fantasy lives our
visions create
Why things happen for a reason, and we meet
our coincidental fates

Dreams and destiny, destiny and dreams
You must be willing to live out one or at least
the other
To eek out the best of life and shift...
from (star) gazer to you, the shining star in the
sky

The Last Car

As it clangs through the track. . .

        moving . . .

along .. . .

          transporting its passengers. . .

. . . It glides along the railways, never to cease
and go back. the ease with which it
follows the rest like a lost soldier.

Behind. . .it stays. . .

      never to lead the way . . .

last are left .. . .

       this car's desires and feelings. . .

Destined will it always be to never spearhead a
journey. Wait, still!. . ...

As the end of the voyage comes with a halt.
Careening.

First is never in the interest of the last car.

Heart in Bloom

The heart is like a delicate flower.
Unfolding to specific traits.
A sun shower here, some shade there.

Aht, aht, aht. Not too much of any ONE thing, it
may upset the flower's balance.
Just like too much pain can do to a heart.
Not enough of any ONE thing can deprive the
flower of vital nutrients.
Not enough LOVE can deprive the heart of
warmth.

If you take care of a flower just right, it can
bloom and grow.
Though sometimes sick, it can easily recuperate.
Just like the heart which goes through ups and
downs.
With some attention, talking to, holding on,
trimming— it can be good.

This is why a heart is like a delicate flower.
Take care of it, and watch it bloom.

Dr. Anne

I am from rice and beans, sirens, gunshots.
Music blasting early Saturday
morning—sometimes Hip-Hop, sometimes
bachata,
ALWAYS a cleaning soundtrack.

I am from Catholic seafood Fridays,
fire hydrant, hot play dates.
I am from Pop, VH1, 90s television.
I am from a full house. "No sleepovers—no
sweet sixteens."

I am from double-shifts, and bus stop waits
with the bestie from around the corner.
I am from dancing in the church.
I am from block parties.

I am from food on the stove.
I am my Tati's trips.
I am the lingering smell of her perfume wafting
down the halls
after she went to work.

I am my Mummy's smile and sociability.
I am hard work. I am fire-crackers.

I am helping Mummy at the laundromat.

I am Toussaint.
I am his absence.
I am Revolution.

I am communions, weddings, funerals.
I am sauce pois and diri a djon jdon.
I am a saint, Perpetua.

I am Yemaya, Oshun, Erzulie, Boukman.
I am free.
I am Grunnie who raised my matriarchs.
I am Goddess.

Empty Plate

Mom made rice, beans, and pepper steak.
So you know I filled my plate—
but I was still hungry when I was done.
I felt like a hole is open.

Sure Mummy put all the love and tenderness in
the food.
She put in me always but that otha side was
missin'.
U know he wasn't there, it's like I was missin' a
meal—
half the love gone cuz u didn't want me.

Did you ever thing to send a card when my
birthday came?
You piece of shit, when you had me did you
even care?
When my mother gave birth did you even know
she was there?

You not just a deadbeat, you're an empty plate.
Neva filled me up, neva gave me food, neva
gave me love.
But you could run around and teach, but its all
bullshit.

You want somme history, study your duty as a
father, as a man.

Cuz you left my mother in front of the stove to
cook the food alone.
It's alright cuz I came out just fine.
Beautiful. free, and okay.
My mom cooked for 2.
Gave me all the love, seasonings, spices and
flavors she could give.
Since you couldn't cook, didn't know how.

I'ma live my life the best I could now.
Never fully full, but I'm still livin, I'm still
breathin'
Cuz my Mummy's rice, beans, and pepper steak
served me well.

An Ode to Dr. Claudine Gay

Doctor to doctor, my heart for you breaks
all the shades of ignorance, for me, a true
intellectual it can't be bliss
Your tenure finished due to the whims of a
zionist—only three years older,
Who's only claim to fame is having a lot of
money, bailing out a mall operator
Somehow his billionaire strings drummed up
stories
That 27 years ago you plagiarized in your
dissertation-OH, the fallacy!

Most lay people have no idea the grit, the drive,
the experiential gauntlet
Required to succumb to academia's lofty pulpit.
They can't even spell plagiarize—don't know
APA, Chicago style, MLA
Yet dumb trigger fingers already ploy to the
media's constant play.

Yo pa konen! Pou jan nou lite na lavi sa,
Pou nou ka réussi, mete famn djamn sou ou
memsi ou pran na mira
Se mwen, pa gen moun kap fe'm kwe
Ke ou te ka ekri mo lot moun, ou pa ta ka vole

Meanwhile, they throw rocks and cast the very
same stones
Of the mediocrity they give and how they've
made it doing far less
Mrs. billionaire ADMITTED to copying from
Wikipedia what a mess!
In everything we do we have to be thrice as
good, vetted 15 times over
And yet when we don't kowtow to their dollars
here comes Massa!

Waving his small endowed intellect, wielding
the biggest part of his dick
His old boys' network, maybe that's it—usually
its the checks largely writ
For six months you were propped up, made
history
But now it's the "shortest tenure in Harvard's
history"

To think you are ALL PWI, that's where we
differ a bit, you and I
I never really wanted to lead them, be a part of
their "coveted" annals
My presence made them better, they couldn't
survive my life's channels
Then again they don't really want diversity,

Just a yes (Black) person, shuckin', jivin'
reflecting moneyed interest subserviently

I'm proud of you either way. When their
ignorance tried to sway, you held it down
In front of your schoolmate who only earned a
Bachelor's she def a clown
They want so bad to create a false narrative, that
it's a "reckoning" they've won
Let them have their shit, watch them burn it,
should be fun
It's always morals this, values that—but in the
face of true intellect they cower

You're still getting paid, your credentials still in
tact
Oh, Dr. Gay but the questions from the peanut
gallery irk my soul it's the attack
I need all the social media "experts" to fall back,
take a knee
Cuz ultimately an academic, rising above the
tide of politics they'll never be

The Makings of The Voluptuary

59 countries in...even my mind is blown at the
thought of all my eyes have seen
I'm not military, not wealthy, just a a girl from
Flatbush who wanted to see

13th century old techniques fortified in cherry
kriek.
The local neighborhood tavern on the corner of
the block.
Closing time, lights on, laughter resounds:
always welcome.
A young Brown girl from Brooklyn, Zomer van
Antwerpen.
An exploration of Europe for the first time ever
Removing the Experiential Lack chip, off my
shoulder.

Walking ancient paths of thousands of years.
Cobblestone pathways,
stone archways, castles come to life looking
over the water.
Building inscriptions on firm foundation,
centuries older than America.

This millennial "non-influencer" on the circular
Wenzel walk of Luxembourg.
One of my first UNESCO joints, the thought that
I must compete with nouveau
riche content creators—actually now that I think
of it, absurd.

Visiting my first European capital of culture,
unlocking loves of artistic ingenuity.
Always making sure in the early days to make
room for cultural history.
Before couch-surfing, hostelling internationally
and timing internet cafe visits.
Tuning into my journalistic inclinations to share
what is transpiring in the wealth of nations.

Snippets of one such email dated from Feb 4,
2012 said:

"Sin Chao! (Hello) as they say here in Vietnam
:-)
. . . .this morning Tomas and I woke up at 4am
and watched the sunrise in the
forest with our guides and we saw some
endangered Gibbon monkies!

City girl Carmen became Jungle Jane (and I
looked like Jane Goodall

too with the green jacket I had on lol) and . .
.you will all be certainly amused
since we spent 5 hours in the jungle and I did it
in slippers. . ."

What a life... Looking back at how tethered I
was.
How many times I tried, planned, organized to
bring people along.
Tried to convince them "Let's go! It's not too bad
if we pay in installments"
The pleathora of itineraries certainly quantifying
the well over 10,000 hours required to be an
expert.

It had to be this way. Solo traveler, the REAL
Carmen, before it was trending.
Taking flight my destiny. What does it all mean?
Being in touch with humans the world over.
Sharing in the common experiences.
Striving to put happiness at the forefront— a
forbidden foray.
That's why it started off on the cheap!
I did at least 30 plus countries on a budget most
wouldn't believe.

Waking up in Kyoto at 6am after taking a (better
than Greyhound) sleeper bus.

Experiencing rows of linear orange details,
walking the path quietly
It's beautiful to be there before throngs of
tourists arrive
Fushimi Inari was a long-awaited prize. Unlike
Angkor Wat, running for my life
Away from the group with the flags and the tour
guide.

To think how the layers of colors laid so
magically
at the top of Rainbow Mountain, after hiking,
little girl me screaming:
Girl you are HIKING, whaaaaaaaaaat?! Flatbush
you, do you SEE?!

That time I climbed a volcano, cursing all the
way.
And how I still keep in touch with one of my
friends along that journey Rai.
It's not a chase, and it's not a thrill really.
Just fulfilling this desire to love God's worldly
works with my presence, openly.

Life's Force

Often written about, it remains to be perhaps the
most common literary subject.
Written about in all kinds of ways, life as it
seems is a mystery of mysteries,
a riddle with no answer.

As Aristotle told of his tragedies, brought on by
the misappropriated virtues
in the lives of his characters.
Others tell of the life of love, bliss, and happily
ever-afters.
A funny think it is—life.

While some things may be predictable,
other things just fall into its schemata.
Like a reevolving door, people come in and go
out.

Some staying longer than others, some leaving
imprints,
some leaving no trace behind. As the door
slows, a main stay lingers.
Never stopping completely, always the activity
of someone or something new.

Much unlike another one of life's major
themes—love.
Life has seldom redundancies or paths that
remain treaded upon continuously.
One of the greatest scientific wonders should be
how lives lived come to pass.

How "time flies when you're having fun,"
how "things change in the blink of an eye,"
how "you've grown!,"
how we all "remember the time when?..."

A marvel to truly be in awe of regardless of how
long or short,
even the comings & goings of life are often
feared, anticipated, induced by some outside
force.

Often moved to a new location or remaining
stagnant in one place.
Regardless of its physical position, life has a
way of sending jolts of lightning.
Shocking the stationary, a way of dropping by
like the unexpected stork,
with bundles of surprises jostling the current
monotonous tides.

Whatever its present mood, whatever its present
occupation,

it is an uncontrollable force, one of God no
doubt.
Some thing that cannot be regulated by the
power of man's technology or science.
Regardless of what new methods are concocted,
there is no denying the true power and
unyielding ways of life.

The Shoe Addiction

I have an addiction with shoes.
I mean a real bad problem. . .
But haven't we all had that (or a similar)
problem though?

You really like these shoes, and they are fly.
You try them on & they're the epitome of your
style, class, sass, pizzazz, you're
zzhhouujjj...Aaaooowww
You go to the mirror and you are even more
intertwined
with this ::smmmmmmmmhhhhhhhh:: amazing
smelling specimen of leather

You have some outfits in the closet.
The bag is set to go & you're ready for a night
on the town with these babies.
You have the money and you could easily go to
the register.
Box in hand, Money Mayweather straight,
you good. . .to. . . go, right??

Well actually, thinkin' about it, ddo you really
NEED them?
I mean when WOULD you wear them?

Everything is copacetic and cool, but. . .
something deep down. . .way down
changes your decision. You decide to leave 'em,
forget about 'em.

You got other stuff to do besides pining away for
'em.
So you walk out the store. . .
Later on you wanna go back and get 'em, but
you don't & you won't.
You just fall back & feel weird + a little empty

Knowing that somebody else is stylin' on 'em +
profilin in them same shoes maybe not even
wearin' 'em properly.

But it's cool you'll make it, you just go on
without those

fly. . .

        sexy. . .

                versatile. .

.

(until you get replaced as a stereotype in my
mind)

pair of shoes.

Love Flame

Confusion is the spark that ignites flames of
illusion.
As Red becomes Orange the transitional phase is
a blur.
Melding so quickly from one shade to the
amalgamated remix
Feelings resonate & begin to spark, in small
flickers.

The coating of Blue's steady light resists this
confusion.
Being the strongest part of the flame it is
headstrong, and
doesn't get warped in the jumbled evolution.

Transformation: from knowing to not knowing;
feeling to no feeling.
As Blue watched this tumultuous conversion —
remains unkeeled
Until the strong blue flame begins to wane and
fall into the confused mess
(Like Upside Down, but more gentrified &
bougie so it's not as bad)

Strong as it was, Blue's flames can no longer
contest
the sanity of the headstrong flame, despite being
— unyielding.
Gives way to insanity, uncertainty, and power
wielding
Red-Orange incomprehensible flame, committed
& diligent—
quickly consumes Blue.

Blue is gone, within the Red-Orange
consummate
now a part, not a whole of just another melded
hue
Yet, cohesiveness has its way.

Just before the spark & flame are gone:
Purple emerges—forming a bond that is
confused.
Yet clear enough to stay...for these few seconds
That short burst of time

Faint, yet strong-enough Purple speaks:
in glitters . . .sparkling. . .shining. . .bright,
#onlyforamoment, #RIP
before it dies.

Weighty Soul

In regards to many different things.
I'm one of those people who SWEAR they don't
want to know too much,
But then read and engage...beyond ENOUGH!

But what is anyone to do, since you HAVE to be
on social media & such
"How will anyone know who you are?"
If it's not there how will I really think YOU
care?

About the consumerism of it all...
I really don't want to shop no more, but ima hit
these scrolls
Then you try to walk away and it's "DISCOUNT
%off SALE"
I gotta stay swagnificient though, if it's good I
may just treat myself.

Is that covered? And did I manage to stay on top
of the 50th person
NOT DOING THEY DAMN JOB!
I called, after I sent the email, after I "waited for
you to get back to me in 2 business days"
because now its another month and a half cuz

I'm tired of chasin behind yo ass. You KNOW
I'm NOT PAYIN'

They wanna hang a skyscraper from an asteroid
that's NEWS.
Migrants are sleepin in schools.
do we really need Elysium?
When the water is DROWNING US EVERY
OTHER WEEK?

I need to make sure I rock this coat though.
Forever 21 isn't really my go to full pricer stop
but this single-item purchase it IT BABY
Cue:: "Ladies is pimps too gon' brush your
shoulders AWWF!"::

The idea I can't win is stuck in my own mind.
But better to have something to reach for and
try.
What else is there to actually do?

It's better to take the path untold
Then think that the bumps & licks along the way
keep hold
Will I ever see my dreams reality?
Or will the latest imperialist, white-settlerr beef
come home to roost and
KABOOOOOOMMMMM!!! Body me?

Gotta stay prayed, stay worded down, observe
all the media bringing out:
THE CLOWNS
Is it ever gonna snow in January again?
Cuz i KNOW that polar ice cap up somewhere
freezing BEEN MELTIN

Will I see my dreams become a reality?
Can the truth ever become the path that others
heed?
You know when all the elders with wisdom are
still on point
and giving society: a READ

Will the road to lies, enshrine the path of deceit?
Weighty soul, I just want to be light.
I aint cause nunna dis mess—
you really need to leave me TF out of it.

The system, the failures, the gaslighting, stop
your bloodclat cryin'!
Wanna be "oppressed so bad"
going after all that you tried to ensure we
NEVER had
It's giving Mariah's (feat. Gucci Mane) 'Why you
so obsessed with me?'

What damage to entire peoples is your
inferiority complex going to cause today?

Pray its not impacting me and mines too crazy
But what future is there if 7 when my son has a
baby?

It's too much going on.
If the asteroid hit at least I had me some damn
fun.
Trying all the things, going to all the places.
Making sure no stone in the passion pit was left
unturned,
if I want to I'ma try it, keep anchored in the
Word.

Weighty Soul trying to get lighter.
The constant negotiation the world trying to
keep you under its thumb
Weighty soul trying to tread lightly
Me, my peace, my joy over everything
And continue to work to spread and catch these
blessings.

Black Excellence

The talented tenth. I studied them so in these
times,
I can appreciate what it meant.
It's kinda sad how deep down low the
consciousness is
I wish reading & critical thinking were TikTok
challenges
But as soon as you try to make it for something
smart
It's corny...all of a sudden.

They were international baby:
Josephine Baker; James Baldwin; Maya
Angelou, Audre Lorde;
Huey P. Newtown somehow they know that the
roots were truly, underground
Connections our ancestors connected long
before to make routes.

Reverting back to the mentalities that undergird
every system we contend with
Only to be told "That's not true" or better yet
"Get over it."
DEI was just a money grab,

you know anything trying to level the playing
field aint gonna last!
We were gettin' way too many jobs, too close to
the decision-makers
A bit too fast. STRIKE IT ALLLLL DOWN.
Beef UP the lynchings and soul crushing acts of
unchecked barbarity.
It's why I never watched Game of Thrones.
They BEEN bloodthirsty on that brown melanin
suffering sadistic shit.

Still I rise, navigating their halls better than Le
Femme Nikita.
At my first job out of undergradd I chose all the
fancy client lunch locations
On them ;-D
"This is such a great choice!" "How did you find
this place?"

Learning that being true to what I love is a
mutually beneficial arrangement.
For the right ones, for MYSELF's fun, for
currency, for love
If my heart's not in it, my principles I won't sell
them
Got it out the mud for real, for real, no cappin'

They say "Self-made," and throw it our faces
making phone calls to cut the line.

Them poppin' in your media, greeting you every
which platform
Poppin' out like Aces to greet ya... like

Ugghhhhh, I'm over you and your rise to star,
banal privileged trajectory
Stealin' cars cuz you're bored, but yeah, you
wanna relate to me.
Congratulations! With all that still NO (real or
worth it to me) personality.
I just can't be bothered with the frivolity.

Well-read, well-spoken, debonaire at large.
Striving, always to reach the stars.
Using the blueprint laid;
Focusing on the ethics and in service to my
talents
The only multitude of ways I consider getting
paid

Sprinkle in the philanthropy magic fairy dust!
Centerpieces, balloons and the bluetooth
speaker.
Tablecloths and accoutrements, the Hostess with
the Mostess
Sho Nuff!!!

Making sure Darkwing Duck, Thundercats &
Gargoyles DVDs intact

When and if I/we gotta "Leave the World
Behind."
Why would I even want to fight, no sushi? No
epic trips? No date nights?
Just survival and whatever iteration of zombies
come to pass?
The world had too much Black Excellence and
squandered it

So I'ma let my star shine bright as hell.
And focus on my freedom with all my might.
Make sure they call me "Doctor" and show some
respect
To the crowning, regal presence of my Black
Excellence.